My Dog Likes To Disco

Funny Poems For Kids

Kenn Nesbitt
Illustrations By Rafael Domingos

Copyright Page from the Original Book

Published by
Purple Room Publishing
1037 NE 65th St #81845
Seattle, WA 98115

Fax: 800-991-2996
ATTN: Purple Room Publishing #81845

www.poetry4kids.com

TABLE OF CONTENTS

For Rhys

My Dog Likes to Disco

My dog likes to disco
on TikTok for fun.
He'd rather start dancing
than go for a run.

My dog likes to wiggle
and jiggle and jump.
He bobbles his noggin
and wriggles his rump.

And when he's done dancing,
this doggy of mine
will pick up his cell phone
and post it online.

2

He puts up a video
once every day
so people can watch
as he wiggles away.

He started on TikTok
for something to do,
but now he's on YouTube
and Instagram too.

He's trending on Twitter
and Facebook as well.
I guess that I should have
been able to tell.

You see, when I rescued
my dog from the pound,
the sign said, "Purebred
social media hound."

My Flat Cat

I have a cat.
My cat is flat.
He sleeps beneath
the bathroom mat.

He slides around
upon the ground
without the slightest
striding sound.

He only eats
the flattest meats
and thin and wispy
kitty treats.

He once was fat
but now my cat
is totally,
completely flat.

He got so slim,
so flat and trim,

the day my Great Dane
sat on him.

Our Dog's Name is Roomba

Our dog's name is Roomba.
He's such a great pup.
If food hits our carpet,
he vacuums it up.

He's constantly sniffing
for food he can "clean."
Our floors are the tidiest
you've ever seen.

There's practically nothing
this puppy won't eat.
He'll munch on the tiniest
morsel of meat.

He'll suck up spaghetti.
He'll polish off peas.
He'll chow down on berries
and cherries and cheese.

He'll lick up linguine.
He'll gobble up grapes.
He'll pig out on pancakes
and waffles and crepes.

The floor in our kitchen
has never been neater.
We're lucky our puppy
is such a good eater.

Our Roomba's a marvelous
morsel remover.
He learned from our other dogs,
Dyson and Hoover.

An Ogre Came Over for Dinner

An ogre came over for dinner.
He showed up with ice cream and cake.
We thought, "It can't hurt,
since he brought us dessert,"
so we asked him to join us for steak.

He crushed the first chair that he sat on.
He busted the table in two.
He ranted and raved
and was badly behaved,
like a rhino escaped from the zoo.

He smashed every plate in the kitchen.
He shattered each saucer and cup.
He broke every bowl.

He was out of control
as he ran around tearing things up.

He broke all the beds in our bedrooms.
He even demolished a door.
He cracked all the walls
in the stairways and halls,
and he left several holes in the floor.

And when he was done causing damage,
although we all wanted to scream,
he said, "That was fun
but I really must run.
I hope you enjoy the ice cream."

I Broke My Mother's iPhone

I broke my mother's iPhone.
I didn't mean to do it.
I played a game that made me mad,
and that was why I threw it.

I tried to fix it quickly.
I used a lot of tape
plus glue and gum and rubber bands
to put it back in shape.

I thought I got it working
but, when I turned it on,
the videos refused to play
and all the games were gone.

It couldn't send an email.
It couldn't send a text.
The apps were mostly missing
which left me quite perplexed.

There wasn't much of anything
her phone could do at all.
The only thing that worked was when
she tried to make a call.

I thought she'd need a brand new phone,
which I would have to get her.
But she just smiled and said, "Hey, thanks!
I think I like this better."

I Let My Sister Cut My Hair

I had to get a haircut.
It was looking much too long.
I let my sister cut it.
I mean, what could she do wrong?

She clipped some bald spots here and there.
She whacked the sides a little.
And then she shaved a three-inch stripe directly down the middle.

She chopped some sections super short,
left others long and wild,
then shaved one eyebrow off before
she looked at me and smiled.

I don't think that I'll let her
give me haircuts anymore.
Or maybe I'll just wait a while;
at least until she's four.

We Ate All the Cheetos

We ate all the Cheetos
and all the Doritos
and all of the chocolates and cheese.
We still have some greens
and a can of sardines
and some pickles and parsnips and peas.

We swallowed the sweets,
all the puddings and treats,
and we finished the ice cream and jam.
What's left is a trout
and a jarful of kraut
and what looks like a turnip or yam.

We drank all the shakes
and we ate all the cakes
and the pies and the fries and the custard.
And yet there's a lime
and a few sprigs of thyme
and a half empty bottle of mustard.

It seems we were hasty
in eating the tastiest
snacks we had purchased before.
Now all that's on hand
is the food we can't stand.
We might have to go to the store.

My Father Can't Find Me

My father can't find me.
He says that it's weird,
I seem to have vanished.
I just disappeared.

My mother can't see me.
She's looking around.
She's calling my name
but I cannot be found.

My brother and sister
both want me to play.
They're searching the house
but I've faded away.

I thought that my family
would all be amused,
but even our dog is
completely confused.

I know it sounds strange
but I'm starting to think
I shouldn't take baths
in invisible ink.

Bradley Bentley Baxter Bloome

Bradley Bentley Baxter Bloome
would never, ever clean his room.
He simply dropped things on the floor
and left them there forevermore.
And even if his parents yelled,
complaining that his bedroom smelled,
and told him, "Bradley Bentley Bloome,
go get a bucket and a broom
and bring them back and clean your room,"
he just refused to pick things up.
So every cord, or coat, or cup,
or Christmas card or candy cane
that hit the floor would just remain.

It only took a little while
before he had a massive pile
of dirty clothes and greasy plates
and dust-encrusted roller skates
and tattered toys and grimy games
and broken bits of picture frames
and rumpled rags and rusted keys
and crumpled bags and cracked CDs
and stuff he'd never seen before
on every inch of bedroom floor.

And even as the clutter grew
with one more muddy, cruddy shoe,
or old and moldy pear or plum,
or sloppy glob of chewing gum,
or burst balloon, or flattened hat,
or battered book, or baseball bat,
or worn and torn up magazine,
still Bradley Bloome would never clean.

He didn't even seem to care
as rubbish covered up his chair,
his desk, his bookcase, and his bed,
and piled up higher than his head,
until, at last, there wasn't room
enough to breathe for Bradley Bloome.
His parents heard him scream and shout,
and tried but couldn't get him out,
because the garbage on the floor
had filled the room and blocked the door.

And, in the end, young Bradley died,
and everyone who knew him cried.
His parents wailed and tore their hair.
His teacher wept in deep despair.
His gran and grandpa grieved and groaned.
His siblings sobbed. His classmates moaned.
His friends all whimpered, "Bradley! Bradley!
Please come back. We miss you badly!"

But, just like kids who came before,
like Godfrey Gordon Gustavus Gore,
the boy who never would shut the door,
and Sarah Cynthia Sylvia Stout,
who would not take the garbage out,
and scrawny little Tawny Skinner,
who could not, would not eat her dinner,
poor Bradley Bentley Baxter Bloome
unfortunately met his doom,
within the grease and grime and gloom
that blocked the door and sealed his tomb.

So, children, if I may assume
you do not want to meet your doom
like Bradley Bentley Baxter Bloome,
go get a bucket and a broom
and bring them back and clean your room.

Cooking Class

I signed up for a cooking class.
I thought it would be fun.
But everything I made came out
completely overdone.

I burned a bowl of noodles.
I set fire to a steak.
I blackened twenty tacos,
seven pizzas, and a cake.

I turned some eggs to ashes and
I torched a piece of toast.
And you don't even want to know
what happened to the roast.

I don't know why but everything
I made went up in smoke.
I even scorched some sushi,
several salads, and a Coke.

My lessons didn't teach me much.
There's just one thing I'm learning:
I'm terrible at cooking,
but I'm excellent at burning.

Sleeping Santa

I woke this Christmas morning
and, much to my surprise,
a sleeping, snoring Santa Claus
was there before my eyes.

It seems he was exhausted
from staying up all night,
delivering his presents on
a long and tiring flight.

He made it to our fireplace
before he fell asleep,

but couldn't take another step
and crumpled in a heap.

And there he slumbered soundly.
He slept the night away,
until I came upon him on
in the hearth on Christmas day.

My puppy started barking.
My sister gave a yell.
But Santa didn't hear a thing
as far as I could tell.

He didn't feel me shake him.
He didn't hear the dog.
So Santa's at our house this morning,
sleeping like a log.

Somebody Stole My Butt

Last night while I was sleeping
somebody stole my butt.
They ran off with my feet and legs.
They even got my gut.

It seems they swiped my elbows;
my arms and shoulders too.
My chest and back have disappeared.
It's really weird, but true.

They made off with my head as well.
They nabbed my neck and throat.
Now all that's left is just my hand.
It's writing you this note.

We're Running Out of Toilet Paper

We're running out of toilet paper.
Paper towels too.
We haven't got much Kleenex left.
I'm not sure what we'll do.

We tried to buy some yesterday.
We went to every shop,
but all the shelves were barren
from the bottom to the top.

We called our friends to see
if they had extra we could borrow,
but they said they have just enough
to last until tomorrow.

Our roll is almost empty now.
A solitary square
is hanging on the holder and
it's way too small to share.

I hope we find some paper soon
or other kinds of wipers.
If not, I'm told I'll have to wear
my baby brother's diapers.

Here's a Silly Poem

Here's a silly poem.
It has lots of silly things.
It has a silly dragon
with a pair of silly wings.
And on the silly dragon
sits a silly little man,
who has no hat, but always wears
a silly frying pan.
And in his silly frying pan
there sits a silly duck
who drives around in circles
in a silly little truck.
And on the silly truck
there is a silly-looking horn
that, every time you squeeze it,
shoots out silly ears of corn.
The fire-breathing dragon
makes the corn begin to pop.
The man can't catch it all,
which means a lot of it will drop.
So if you ever see it
raining popcorn from the sky,
look up and you might see
a silly dragon flying by.

I'm Keeping My Distance

I'm keeping my distance from people today.
I'm trying to stay at least six feet away.

I'm not shaking hands now, or giving high fives
to try to make sure everybody survives.

I'm wearing a face mask and gloves and a gown.

I'm staying at home. I'm not out on the town.

I'm washing my hands every hour or two,
because I'm convinced it's the right thing to do

since someone at school kissed me right on the cheek
and gave me a case of the cooties this week.

My Dog Likes to Dig

My dog likes to dig, making holes in our lawn.
He digs every morning beginning at dawn.
He digs like a maniac all afternoon,
and even at night by the light of the moon.

I wish he would stop but he's out of control,
and works up a sweat digging hole after hole.
He's fevered and frenzied. He's hot as can be.
His temperature's rising degree by degree.

His workout from digging is clearly extreme.

He's sizzling. He's scorching. He's starting
to steam.
I wish I had gotten a fish or a frog.
Instead I just have this hot diggity dog.

On Halloween Night

A couple of demons,
on Halloween night,
showed up on my doorstep
to give me a fright.

I smiled when I saw them.
I gave them a wink,
and handed them each
a delicious, cold drink.

You might think it's weird
but I wasn't afraid.
When life gives me demons
I make demonade.

Sunday's Somewhat Melancholy

Sunday's somewhat melancholy.
Monday's slightly sad.
Tuesday's quite disheartening.
Wednesday's just as bad.
Thursday's filled with gloominess.
Friday's rather glum.
I wish it didn't take a week
for Saturday to come.

Coming Soon!

I'm building a rocket to launch into space,
to fly to the moon and all over the place.
It's practically finished. It's nearly all done.
If you want to come we'll have oodles of fun.

You'll just need a ticket reserving your place
for once-in-a-lifetime adventures in space.
The tickets right now are just fifty apiece.
But, next month, I'm sure that the cost will increase.

This voyage will be an unqualified smash,
so, line up right here and I'll take all your cash.
And, once I've collected a million or more,
I'll finish the rocket we'll use to explore.

I promise that I will return really soon
to take everyone on that trip to the moon.
But what if I can't make it work?
Never fear...
Your ticket will still make a great souvenir.

My Mother Drives Me Everywhere

My mother drives me everywhere.
She drives me to my school.
She drives me to my football practice
and the swimming pool.

She drives me to piano lessons,
and my English tutor.
She drives me to the mall to get
new games for my computer.

She'd rather that I rode my bike,
or walked, or took the bus.
But if she doesn't drive me
I just whine and make a fuss.

I'd get around without her but
I'm really much too lazy.
My mother drives me everywhere
and I just drive her crazy.

After Thanksgiving

It's after Thanksgiving.
I'm full as can be.
I haven't got room left
for even a pea.

I probably gobbled
too much at our feast.
I'm straining in pain and
my waistline's increased.

I'm utterly glutted.
My stomach is stuffed.
My belly is bulging.

My tummy is puffed.

I'm totally bloated.
I'm huffing and puffing.
I guess it's not smart to eat
nothing but stuffing.

I Think I'm in Love with My Smartphone

I think I'm in love with my smartphone.
I've never felt this way before.
I used to be lonely without it.
I don't feel alone anymore.

My phone is my constant companion.
It loves to just hang out and play.
As long as I plug it in nightly,
it charms and delights me all day.

It likes to play music and movies.
It never says no to a game.
It answers my questions so sweetly.
Without it, life isn't the same.

I hope you don't misunderstand me
or think that I'm some kind of freak,
but I fell in love with my smartphone,
so we're getting married next week.

I Have a Bunch of Batteries

I have a bunch of batteries
I need to give away,
and, if you'd like to have them,
you can get them all today.

I didn't want to throw them out.
They're yours to take instead.
I probably should warn you, though,
these batteries are dead.

I have a lot of tiny ones.
A few of them are large.
And you can have them all right now,
completely free of charge.

A Real Groaner

I stood in line to get some punch.
I wanted some to drink with lunch.
The line was long. The line was slow.
It seemed to take an hour or so.
At last I got up to the front.
The serving lady gave a grunt
and punched me squarely on the nose,
which made me groan. That's how it goes.
I shook my head. I should have known...
A punchline sure can make you groan.

Switch Switch

My little brother took my Switch
to stream a game or two on Twitch.
But, when he tried to turn it on,
my Switch would not play Pokémon.

My Switch would not play Mario,
or Donkey Kong, or Yu-Gi-Oh!,
or Minecraft, or Monopoly,
or Captain Toad, or Pikmin 3,
Jurassic Park, or Kingdom Hearts,
or any game with racing karts,
or Shovel Knight, or Dragon Ball,
or, really, any game at all.

He gave it back and said, “It’s broke.”
I had to giggle at my joke.
I switched my Switch and played a trick.
I’d given him my painted brick.

Liverwurst Pie

Liverwurst Pie, oh, Liverwurst Pie.
The first time I tried it I thought I would die.
It tasted disgusting. I couldn't say why.
I just knew I didn't like Liverwurst Pie.

Liverwurst Pie, oh, Liverwurst Pie.
The next time I tried it I started to cry.
It wasn't as bad as the first time, but why
would anyone ever eat Liverwurst Pie?

The third time I tried it I thought, my oh my,
I don't think I'll die, and I won't even cry.
But still, I would tell you that I'm not a guy

who ever would learn to like Liverwurst Pie.

The fourth time I tried it—I won't tell a lie—
I started to like eating Liverwurst Pie.
It tasted so good that I went out to buy
another big serving of Liverwurst Pie.

Liverwurst Pie, oh, Liverwurst Pie.
It might take a few times before you don't cry.
But I recommend that you give it a try,
and, really, I mean it ... I hope you don't die.

A Goat in a Landfill

A goat was in a landfill
eating garbage and debris
and came across a movie;
a discarded DVD.

He chewed the case and cover
and the flavor made him smile.
He took the disc between his lips
and nibbled for a while.

He thought, "This film is brilliant;
full of action and suspense.
The story is exciting
and the fight scenes are intense.

"It's got a lot of comedy,
a touch of sweet romance,
and music so inspiring
it makes me want to dance."

He gnawed a little longer
through some drama and a chase,
and finished off the movie
with a grin upon his face.

He gulped the closing credits—
one more bite was all it took—
and thought, "That film was awesome
but I still preferred the book."

Frank, the Friendly Alien

I'm Frank, the friendly alien.
from deepest outer space.
My face is fairly friendly.
It's such a friendly face.

My teeth are sharp and pointed.
My eyes are big and red.
I have such friendly features
upon my friendly head.

My horns are green and shiny.
I have exactly three.
My nose is long and crooked,
the way a nose should be.

My ears are huge and scaly.
My tongue is brown and blue.
The people from my planet
all look friendly like I do.

My claws are shaped like daggers.
My hands are huge and hairy
I'd love to stay and tell you more
but you look much too scary.

A Centaur Goes out Shopping

There's nothing like a shopping spree
to elevate my mood;
the joy of filling shopping carts with
clothing, toys and food.

I'm something of a clotheshorse;
I can never have enough.
I go out shopping every day
to buy a bunch more stuff.

I hang around the shopping mall
and corner grocery store.
I'm fond of farmers markets
and garage sales I adore.

I love the thrill of bargain hunting.
Sales are oh so nice.
You'll find I frequent flea marts
just to haggle over price.

So if you'd like to learn to shop
but find you need a mentor,
I hope you'll come and visit me
for I'm The Shopping Centaur.

A Tiny, Spiny Dinosaur

A tiny, spiny dinosaur
was racing through my house;
a tiny, spiny dinosaur
no bigger than a mouse.

That tiny, spiny dinosaur,
it leapt up on my bed.
It punched me in the stomach
and it hit me on the head.

It chased me from my bedroom
and pursued me down the stairs.
It knocked the TV over
and it broke a pair of chairs.

I don't know where it came here from
or how it got inside.
The only thing I know is that
I need a place to hide.

I'll have to catch that dinosaur
before it gets too late.
But, oh, it found my brother's room...
I guess that I can wait.

Speak when this Way Talk Do I

Speak when this way talk do I
so, if converse do we,
you'll talk to need to this way try
to talk with have a me.

It strange may somewhat first at sound
but for it try a bit.
It's this way fun I've talk to found.
I've done my life all it.

It's understand to hard know I
but and you'll try it see.
If sideways talk you can to try,
it's talk with fun to me.

Book Storm

I wasn't doing anything,
just lying on my bed,
when my dictionary tumbled down
and smacked me on the head.

Then Harry Potter toppled off,
and Judy Moody too.
I almost got knocked out by
Wimpy Kid and Nancy Drew.

Then Fancy Nancy whacked me.
All those Goosebumps were intense;

they landed with A Series
of Unfortunate Events.

So now I'm in a pile of books.
It's something of a shame.
This never should have happened.
I have just my shelf to blame.

My Brother just Eats Candy

My brother just eats candy
and my sister just eats cakes.
The only thing my mother likes
are double-chocolate shakes.

My dad devours danishes
and donuts by the dozen.
My aunt and uncle live on pie
exactly like my cousin.

My grandpa and my grandma
just drink soda pop and punch.
My nephew and my niece
eat cookies every day for lunch.

And me, I'll dine on any kind
of sugar-covered treat.
My family isn't healthy, but
we sure are awfully sweet.

My Legs Both Understand Me

My legs both understand me.
My shoulders have my back.
My arms are always on my side.
My feet know I'm on track.

My hands are both forgiving,
and help me seize the day.
My ears are awesome listeners.
My eyes see things my way.

My bottom is behind me.
My hair sticks up for me.
My fingers give me two thumbs up.
My smile won't disagree.

My bones are so supportive.
My veins are all true-blue.
My legs both understand me.
I hope that you do too.

Cheese Breeze

Whenever I eat dairy,
it makes me have to toot.
You might think that sounds scary.
I think it's kind of cute.

A sip of milk, some butter,
a tiny bit of cheese,
will make my tummy flutter
and cause a "bottom breeze."

An ice cream cone or custard,
some yogurt or some ghee,

and then that noise you just heard...
That probably was me.

You might think I'm unlucky.
You might think it's unfair.
But I don't find it yucky;
it's just my dairy air.

I Don't Watch TV

I don't watch TV.

I mean, who's got the time?

I only watch YouTube,
and Netflix, and Prime,
and Hulu, and Crackle,
and Roku, and Tubi,
and Vudu, and Hoopla,
and Yahoo, and Mubi,
and Google, and Apple,
and Vimeo too,
and Disney, and PopcornFlix.

That's all I do.

There's so much to stream!

It might seem like a crime
to not watch TV,
but, then, who's got the time?

How to Make People Like You

I got a new book.
You should come take a look.
It's called, "How to Make People Like You."
I read it today
to see what it would say,
and I did what it told me to do.

I read the directions
in all of the sections.
I followed them all one by one.
I thought, when this ends,
I'll have so many friends,
and that would be awesome and fun.

The steps were correct,

but I didn't expect
it would have me complaining and groaning.
I made people like me,
but what didn't strike me,
is this was a book about cloning.

The Story of Laurie

Perhaps you shouldn't read this story.
It isn't sweet and hunky-dory.
It isn't even just okay,
or nice or kind in any way.
In fact, it's gruesome, grim, and gory,
and all about a girl named Laurie.

See, Laurie is a cannibal.
She'll eat no plant nor animal.
She'll eat no vegetable nor fruit,
no leaf, no seed, no sprout, nor shoot.
And if you offer fish or fowl

she'll stare at you and start to growl.

It's not that Laurie's mean or mad.
She simply thinks that beans are bad.
She says, "No thanks" to chips and cheese,
bologna, carrots, parsley, peas,
bananas, bagels, sauerkraut,
arugula and rainbow trout.

She doesn't care for Christmas roast,
or pie or pumpernickel toast,
or rigatoni, ravioli,
mustard, custard, guacamole,
pickles, yogurt, sirloin steak,
or even candy bars and cake.

She'll never feed on frozen food.
And any entree, steamed or stewed,
from any package, box, or bag,
is guaranteed to make her gag.
It's not part of her diet plan;
the only thing she eats is Man.

I truly hope I never meet
with Laurie, for I know she'll eat
my feet, my legs, my arms, my head,
and then, of course, I'll end up dead.
And that's the one thing I would hate:
To be the poet Laurie ate.

I Got a New Laptop for Christmas

I got a new "laptop" for Christmas.
It's awesome and couldn't be cuter.
It isn't a regular laptop.
It isn't some kind of computer.

This laptop's not battery-powered.
It's missing a keyboard and screen.
It doesn't connect to the wi-fi.
It's not some device or machine.

And, yet, I'm in love with my laptop.
You might even say that I'm smitten.
I asked for a laptop for Christmas,
so Santa Claus brought me a kitten.

My Project for the Science Fair

My project for the Science Fair
was absolutely cool.
I built myself a time machine
and showed it off at school.

Inventing it was not too hard;
I had a little aid.
My future self came back in time
and showed me how they're made.

Lonely Phone

My phone must be
a lonely phone.
It often does things
on its own.

It likes to blink
and buzz and beep
to wake me up
when I'm asleep.

I sometimes find
it's made a call
without me touching
it at all.

If it gets bored,
before too long,
it might decide
to play a song,

or maybe shoot
a video,
or send a tweet,

or watch a show,

or play a game,
or type a text.
I never know
what's coming next.

Today I left
my phone at home.
While I was gone
it wrote this poem.

The Candy Cane Collector

Hello, my name is Hector.
I'm a candy cane collector.
I collect the finest candy canes
from all around the world.

My candy canes are quite a sight.
While some are dark and some are light,
they're mostly colored red and white,
and all of them are swirled.

A few of them are blue or green,
or purple, pink, or tangerine,
or pumpkin-hued for Halloween,
or rainbow-colored too.

I go to countries far and near
to buy them all and bring them here,
three hundred sixty days a year.
It's what I like to do.

I tour the world on ships and planes,
and buses, bikes, and subway trains
because collecting candy canes
has always been my mission.

I hope you'll come and see someday.
I've set them out. They're on display.
And, best of all, I have to say,
they're all in mint condition.

I Washed Our Dad's Car

I washed our dad's car with my sister,
to clean off the grime and the grunge.
My sister got mad and
complained to our dad and
asked, "Why can't he just use a sponge?"

My Mirror Likes to Argue

My mirror likes to argue.
He likes to fight and feud.
He often disagrees with me.
He's regularly rude.

He's fond of making faces.
He loves to sneer and scowl.
And, if I scream and shout at him,
he'll holler, hoot, and howl.

I wish I'd never met him.
I wish he'd go away.
I wish I didn't chance upon him
several times a day.

I think perhaps the next time
he starts to disagree,
I'll smile at him to see if maybe
he'll be nice to me.

I Like Myself the Way I Am

I like myself the way I am.
I'm really glad I'm me.
In fact, I'm sure there's no one else
on Earth I'd rather be.

I'd rather not be someone else.
I wouldn't want to switch,
unless they were more beautiful,

or powerful, or rich.

I only want to be myself.
To change would just be wrong,
except if they were super smart,
or muscular and strong.

Unless they were more talented,
or glamorous, or tall,
or popular, or interesting,
I'd never change at all.

Except if they were famous or
had won the lottery,
I'd like to stay the way I am.
I'm glad to just be me.

My Family's Fond of Gadgets

My family's fond of gadgets
and new technology.
My mother likes her radio.
My father likes TV.

My sister likes to dance around
the house with headphones on.
My brother plays on his PC
until the break of dawn.

The baby has a smartphone
and a touchscreen-tablet too.
If we had pets, I'm sure
that even they would have a few.

We chat with instant messaging.
We email and we text.
We're always looking forward
to the gadget we'll get next.

The power went out recently.
That day was like no other.
Our screens went blank and, strange but true,
we talked to one another.

One Warm, Sunny Day

One warm, sunny day
on a cold, snowy night,
the inky-black darkness
was sunny and bright.

The evening that morning—
that midnight at noon—
was late in December,
one April in June.

I stood where I sat
as I ran, lying still,
deep down in a valley
on top of a hill.

The people beside me
were nowhere around.
The birds in the sky were
all deep underground.

The fish in the tree
were asleep in their nest,
and watched the sun set
as it rose in the west.

Yes, that's what I saw
when my eyes were closed tight,
one warm, sunny day
on a cold, snowy night.

My Mother Took Me to the Mall

My mother took me to the mall
to visit Old Saint Nick.
She wanted me upon his knee
to snap our yearly pic.

We do it every Christmas but,
this year, I changed my mind.
I thought I'd like a photo
of a slightly different kind.

I didn't sit on Santa's lap
or climb up on his chair
despite the fact that Santa was
the reason we were there.

Instead, I grabbed my mother's phone
and ran up to an elf
and snapped a photograph
with Santa's helper and myself.

My mother looked confused
but I just grinned from ear to ear
and said, "I took an elfie
for my Christmas pic this year."

My iPhone Did My Homework

My iPhone did my homework.
I simply talked to Siri.
I read her all the problems
and she answered every query.

I asked her, "What is five times twelve?"
She answered, "Allentown."
Her answer seemed suspicious
but I shrugged and wrote it down.

I asked her, "Who's the President
or leader of Peru?"
She answered, "Forty seven,"
so I wrote that one down too.

I asked her ten more questions,
and she answered every one.
Her answers seemed bizarre
but I was glad to have it done.

It seems that Siri's not too smart,
or maybe slightly deaf.
I turned my homework in today
and got a big, red "F."

I guess, for homework,
Siri's not the best to call upon.
I'll only let Alexa
do my homework from now on.

Chocolate for Breakfast

Chocolate for breakfast.
Chocolate for lunch.
Chocolate for dinner.
Chocolate for brunch.

Chocolate on Saturday,
chocolate on Sunday,
and nothing but chocolate
the whole day on Monday.

On Tuesday and Wednesday
it's chocolate galore.
On Thursday and Friday
I eat even more.

I know it's not healthy;

that's totally clear.
But, still, I go nuts in
November each year.

And there's not a fruit
or a veggie in sight
at least for a week
after Halloween night.

The Football Game Is on TV

The football game is on TV.
The chips are in the bowl.
We're totally excited and
about to lose control.

Our living room has turned into
a huge, chaotic scene.
We're madly jumping up and down.
We're screaming at the screen.

My mom and dad are yelling
while my baby brother wails.
My sister's sitting on the sofa
chewing on her nails.

I'm running all around the room
as if I've lost my mind.
It's not because our team's ahead.
It's not that they're behind.

The reason that we're shouting
and we're running all about
is that the game was tied and then
the Internet went out.

I Made a Meme this Morning

I made a meme this morning.
I posted it online.
(I asked my mom's permission.
She said that it was fine.)

Then people started sharing it.
The next thing that I knew,
my meme had spread around the world.
It grew, and grew, and grew!

By lunch my meme went viral.
It had a billion views.
By dinnertime the TV had it

on the evening news.

I earned a penny, maybe two,
from every single share,
and, by the time I went to bed,
I was a millionaire.

I thought of making one more meme
that might go even higher.
But, nah, I'm nearly nine years old.
I think I'll just retire.

And Backed My Car into a Tree

and backed my car into a tree.
I wrote this poem back to front
or else you may end up like me.
So do not try this silly stunt,

I'm stunned and don't know what to say.
Now things could not be any worse.
while driving in my car today.
I wrote this poem in reverse

Backward Dan

.man backward the Dan Backward I'm
.can you if me with backward Rhyme
.down goes sun the when up wake I
.frown a wears, happy when, face My
.dessert for dinner my eat I
.shirt a like just wear I pants My
.dad and mom my than older I'm
.sad I'm when laughing always I'm
.can you if me with backward Rhyme
.man backward the Dan Backward I'm

I Made a Wish

I found a lamp. A dirty lamp.
I rubbed it to a shine.
A genie from the lamp said he
would grant a wish of mine.

I made a wish. A simple wish.
It practically came true.
I wished I had a million dollars
and a pickle too.

I got the million dollars,
but I really can't say why
I never got the pickle.

I think I'm going to cry.

I'd Like to Be a Movie Star

I'd like to be a movie star.
I'd do it if I could.
I'd pack up my belongings and
I'd move to Hollywood.

As soon as I arrived there,
I would make my screen debut.
I'd star in flashy action films.
Adventure movies too.

I'd be in countless comedies
to make the viewers laugh.
Then, when they saw me on the street,
they'd want my autograph.

I'd soon become so famous
that the world would know my name.
I'd hang out with celebrities
and join the Hall of Fame.

I'd buy a fancy mansion
on an island paradise.
I'd love to be a movie star.
Oh, wouldn't that be nice.

There's just one little problem;
just one complicating fact...
My parents tell me every day
I don't know how to act.

Vacation Cancellation

My parents have canceled our summer vacation.
We won't take our road trip and travel the nation.
We're staying at home for the total duration,
and will not be leaving this single location.
They said that the name of this strange situation
is something that's known as a family "staycation."

You might think that I would be feeling frustration
or some other similar sorry sensation.
But I'm feeling nothing but joy and elation,
and giving my parents a standing ovation.
You see, what this means is, by my calculation,
I'll have the whole summer to play my Playstation.

I Woke up this Morning

I woke up this morning.
I climbed out of bed.
I put on my clothes
and a hat on my head.

I went to the kitchen
to look for some food.
I let out a yawn,
then I sleepily chewed.

I picked up my books
and my lunch and a snack
and managed to stuff it
all into my pack.

I walked out the front door
and wandered to school,
and, wow, did I feel like
the world's biggest fool.

The lights were all off
and the doors were all locked,
and I was embarrassed;
a little bit shocked.

I looked at my watch
and, indeed, it was eight.
But I'd overslept.
I was twelve hours late.

Thank You, Thanksgiving

Thank you, Thanksgiving.
We're glad that you're here.
You ring in this season
of holiday cheer.

You give us a day to
express gratitude
with family and friends and
a whole bunch of food;

with turkey and gravy

and green beans and hams
and cranberry sauce
and potatoes and yams.

Regarding desserts
you are second to none.
So, thank you, Thanksgiving!
You're festive and fun.

But, mostly, Thanksgiving,
you're totally cool
because you're a couple
of days off from school.

Yesterday I Took a Test

Yesterday I took a test.
I got a perfect score.
A perfect score is something
that I've never had before.

My teacher nearly fainted.
My parents were impressed
to think that I knew every single
answer on the test.

But that's not how I did it.
No, it was only luck.
I guessed on every answer;
not just ones where I was stuck.

I guess it was my lucky day.
I feel like such a fool.
I should have played the lottery.
Instead, I went to school.

My Favorite Word Is "Floofy"

My favorite word is "floofy." It's such a floofy word.
In fact, I'd say that floofy
is the floofiest I've heard.

I use it when I'm floofing up,
or when I'm all floofed out.
Whenever I feel floofy-doof
I give a floofy shout!

I may not know what floofy means.
But—floofy!—that's okay.
I'm sure it's floofy floofy floof
to floof it anyway.

I know it might sound silly.
I know it might sound goofy.
But, still, there's not another word
that's floofier than floofy.

Basketball Is Lots of Fun

Basketball is lots of fun.
It's my favorite sport.
But I'm so bad that, when I play,
they throw me off the court.

Now hockey is my favorite sport.
The trouble is I stink.
So every time I hit the ice
they throw me off the rink.

Now soccer is the game I like.
There's just one little hitch:
I kick and run too slow, and so
they throw me off the pitch.

At last, I found some sports that I
can play and not get thrown.
I now play soccer, basketball,
and hockey on my phone.

A Hippo Is Bounding Around on My Head

A hippo is bounding around on my head.
Gorillas are banging on drums.
A rhino is charging me full speed ahead
while a crocodile's eyeing my thumbs.

A rattlesnake's winding his way up my side.
A tiger is sniffing my clothes.
A grizzly just grabbed me, his mouth open wide.
A tarantula's perched on my nose.

I'm drowning, surrounded by man-eating sharks.
An elephant sits on my chest.

Yes, that's how it feels when the teacher remarks,
"Grab your pencils. It's time for the test."

A Goat from Minnesota

A goat from Minnesota
met a goat from Manitoba
on the border near a forest
on the shoreline of a bay.

Said the goat from Manitoba
to the goat from Minnesota,
"I got lost. Are we in Canada
or in the U.S., eh?"

Today I Wore a Costume

Today I wore a costume so
I looked just like a parrot.
And yesterday I dressed up as
a giant, talking carrot.

The day before, my costume was
a life-sized Pikachu.
And, earlier, a superhero,
and a kangaroo.

Tomorrow I expect that I
will be a dinosaur
and tromp around the house so

everyone can hear me roar.

It's not because it's Halloween.
I won't be trick-or-treating.
No, I just like to photobomb
Mom's daily online meeting.

I'm Super Excited!

I'm super excited,
as if I could fly.
I'm so overjoyed that
I nearly could cry.

It's such a sensation
I'm having today.
I'm whooping and cheering
and shouting, "Hooray!"

A weight on my shoulders
was instantly lifted.
It suddenly seems like
a gift I've been gifted.

My mood is improving.
My spirits are lighter.
It feels like the future
is bound to be brighter.

The spring in my step
is apparent to all.
My head is held high and
I'm standing up tall.

I'm cheerful and chipper.
I'm happy-go-lucky.
I'm tickled to tell you
I'm feeling just ducky.

I'm thrilled. I'm elated.
I'm yelling, "Yahoo!"
And, what's more important,

I hope you are too.

This Winter I Went Sledding

This winter I went sledding.
I crashed into a tree.
I ran into another one
while learning how to ski.

I slipped upon the sidewalk.
(I didn't see the ice.)
A snowball hit me in the face.
(My sister's not too nice.)

My snowman toppled over.
It landed on my head.
My tongue got frozen to a pole.

I pulled it off. It bled.

I froze my toes and fingers.
They hurt so much I cried.
So, yes, the snow is pretty,
but I think I'll stay inside.

Don't Forget to Floss

The dentist told me, "Brush your teeth,
and don't forget to floss."
I promised I would do it
and told him, "You're the boss!"

When I got home, I brushed my teeth,
then found the perfect stance.
I swung my hips and swept my arms
as I began to dance.

I wiggled back and forth until
I figured I was through.
I'm really glad the dentist told me
that's what I should do.

Now every time I brush, I floss.
It's fun, but I don't see
how dancing after brushing
can prevent a cavity.

Bob's Job

My name is Bob. I have a job.
My job is crushing cans,
like Coca Cola, 7Up,
and lots of other brands.

I flatten cans from Mr. Pibb,
and Dr. Pepper too,
Sierra Mist, and RC Cola,
Sprite, and Mountain Dew.

I whack them with a hammer or

I beat them with a bat,
to pound the Pepsi, squash the Squirt,
and press the Fresca flat.

I mash the cans from Fanta
and from A&W.
It may look like I'm happy,
but that, sadly, isn't true.

My work is pretty boring
which, at times, I find distressing.
But that's what always happens
when your job is soda pressing.

Whenever It's December

Whenever it's December
and I think about the year,
both the one that's almost over
and the one that's nearly here,

I recall how, in the springtime,
all of nature was transformed,
as the flowers started blooming
and the winter weather warmed.

Then the summer followed springtime;
how the months went by so fast!
I had thought the long and sunny days
would last, and last, and last.

But the summer turned to autumn
and the leaves began to blow.
I could tell that pretty soon
we would be blanketed in snow.

Now it's once again December
and the days are growing colder.
I'm another twelve months wiser
and another twelve months older.

And I dream about the new year
and the old one I remember.
It's the way I like to celebrate
whenever it's December.

ABOUT THE AUTHOR

Children's Poet Laureate (2013-2015) Kenn Nesbitt is the author of many books for children, including *The Armpit of Doom, More Bears!, The Tighty-Whitey Spider,* and *One Minute Till Bedtime.* He is also the creator of the world's most popular children's poetry website, www.poetry4kids.com.

More Books by Kenn Nesbitt

One Minute Till Bedtime – It's time for tuck-in, and your little one wants just one more moment with you–so fill it with something that will feed the imagination, fuel a love of reading, and send them off to sleep in a snap! Little Brown Books for Young Readers.

Bigfoot Is Missing – Children's Poets Laureate J. Patrick Lewis and Kenn Nesbitt team up to offer a smart, stealthy tour of the creatures of shadowy myth and fearsome legend. Bigfoot, the Mongolian Death Worm, and the Loch Ness Monster number among the many creatures lurking within these pages. Chronicle Books.

Believe it or Not, My Brother Has a Monster – From one scary monster to ten disgusting slugs and everything in between, this spooky story is full of creepy crawlies ... and one nervous little brother! Scholastic.

Kiss, Kiss Good Night – Snuggle up with this bedtime poem, all about how mommy animals say good night to their little ones. Cartwheel Books.

My Cat Knows Karate – Another seventy poems about goofy gadgets, kooky characters, funny families, insane situations, and much, much more.

The Biggest Burp Ever – Seventy more poems about wacky animals, comical characters, funny families, silly situations, and much, much more.

The Armpit of Doom – Seventy new poems about crazy characters, funny families, peculiar pets, comical creatures, and much, much more.

The Ultimate Top Secret Guide to Taking Over the World – Are you fed up with people telling you what to do? You're in luck. Just read this book and in no time at all you will be laughing maniacally as the world cowers before you. Sourcebooks Jabberwocky.

MORE BEARS! – Kenn Nesbitt's picture book debut will have you laughing while shouting "More Bears!" along with the story's disruptive audience. Sourcebooks Jabberwocky.

The Tighty-Whitey Spider: And More Wacky Animals Poems I Totally Made Up – With poems like and "I Bought Our Cat a Jetpack" and "My Dog Plays Invisible Frisbee," this collection shines with rhymes that are full of jokes, thrills, and surprises. Sourcebooks Jabberwocky.

My Hippo Has the Hiccups: And Other Poems I Totally Made Up- *My Hippo Has the Hiccups* contains over one hundred of Kenn's newest and best-loved poems. The dynamic CD brings the poems to life with Kenn reading his own poetry, cracking a joke or two, and even telling stories about how the poems came to be. Sourcebooks Jabberwocky.

Revenge of the Lunch Ladies: The Hilarious Book of School Poetry – From principals skipping school to lunch ladies getting back at kids who complain about cafeteria food, school has never been so funny. Meadowbrook Press.

When the Teacher Isn't Looking: And Other Funny School Poems – *When the Teacher Isn't Looking* may be the funniest collection of poems about school ever written. This collection of poems by Kenn Nesbitt is sure to have you in stitches from start to finish. Meadowbrook Press.

The Aliens Have Landed at Our School! – No matter what planet you live on, this book is packed with far-out, funny, clever poems guaranteed to give you a galactic case of the giggles. Meadowbrook Press.

For more funny poems, visit
www.poetry4kids.com

Back Cover Material

MY DOG
LIKES TO DISCO

Kenn Nesbitt, possible the funniest poet ever to wield a pen, is back with more of the impossible poems, outrageous rhymes, and absurd wordplay that kids can't stop reading.

My Dog Likes to Disco unleashes seventy new poems about disco-dancing dogs, invisible kids, misbehaving phones, preposterous people, and much, much more.

Be sure to visit Kenn online at the world's most popular poetry site for kids: www.poetry4kids.com

Index

V

W

Y

www.ingramcontent.com/pod-product-compliance
Lightning Source LLC
Chambersburg PA
CBHW021238090426
42740CB00006B/592

* 9 7 8 1 0 3 8 7 6 3 5 7 0 *